WOMEN LIKE ME

Community

Sharing Words of Gratitude

COMPILED BY JULIE FAIRHURST

To Marilyn,
Destiny is not a matter of chance! It is a matter of choice!
Love
Donna Fairhurst

WOMEN LIKE ME
COMMUNITY

SHARING WORDS OF GRATITUDE

JULIE FAIRHURST

X O X O

ROCK STAR PUBLISHING

CONTENTS

Do You Listen To Your Dreams?   ix
Introduction   xiii

PART 1
SHARING WORDS OF GRATITUDE

1. JENNIFER SPARKS   3
2. LINDA FOOTE   11
3. LORETTA LEBRETON   17
4. LEANNE GIAVEDONI   21
5. PAULINE AWINO ATITWA   25
6. SHERON CHISHOLM   29
7. JANICE RENSHAW   33
8. KIM KORBLE   37
9. BARBARA KISILOSKI   39
10. ANNE-MARIE HARRIS   43
11. MARISA LAVALLEE   47
12. TRISH SCOULAR   51
13. LINDA S. NELSON   55
14. BRENDA COOPER   59
15. DONNA FAIRHURST   63
16. SABRINA LAMBERT   67
17. DANA K. CARTWRIGHT   71
18. ERICA DENNIS   75
19. SHERI GODFREY   79
20. THERESA CROWLEY   83
21. LYNDSEY SCOTT   87
22. SUSAN DABORN   91
23. MICHELLE VOYAGEUR   95
24. COLINDA LAVIOLETTE   99
25. KIM MALLORY   103
26. IRENE SUTHERLAND   107

27. HEATHER SCOTT   109

28. JULIE BREAKS   113

29. GRATITUDE LESSON   117

30. YOUR MINDSET MATTERS   123

31. CONFIDENCE JOURNAL   131

32. THANK YOU TO THE WLM   · 133
COMMUNTIY

PART 2
LEARN MORE ABOUT WOMEN LIKE ME

33. JOIN THE WOMEN LIKE ME   137
COMMUNITY

34. KIND WORDS FROM WLM AUTHORS   139

35. MEET JULIE FAIRHURST   143

36. IS IT TIME FOR YOU TO BECOME A   147
PUBLISHED AUTHOR

37. CONNECT WITH ME   151

Also by Julie Fairhurst   155

www.womenlikemestories.com

...

HENRY WARD BEECHER

"The unthankful heart discovers no mercies; but let the thankful heart sweep through the day and, as the magnet finds the iron, so it will find, in every hour, some heavenly blessings."

DO YOU LISTEN TO YOUR DREAMS?

In 2016, I was searching for my purpose and struggling to continue the pace of my extremely successful real estate career. A career that has spanned over 30 years. I loved my career, and the over 2,500 clients I'd helped over the years. However, I'd lost my way and I knew it was time for more. But what?

One night as I slept, in the middle of the night, I experienced a profound life-changing dream.

I was being led back from wherever I was, and I remember saying, "No, I don't want to go back, I want to stay here with you." I was told, "No you must go back you are not finished yet."

I felt so confused and sad as I really wanted to stay, wherever I was at that moment. "But I don't know my purpose," I cried out. I was then told, "You, you are your purpose."

I remember feeling anxious and saying, "I don't know what to do."

I was told one word, "Write!"

Welcome to Women Like Me

Julie Fairhurst

...

GERMANY KENT

"It's a funny thing about life, once you begin to take note of the things you are grateful for, you begin to lose sight of the things that you lack."

INTRODUCTION

Learning about gratitude and being grateful in my life was one of the most life changing lessons I could have ever learnt. When you grow up in chaos and negativity is all that is shown to you as a young child, it is difficult to accept gratitude into your life. However, it is imperative that you do if you want to live a full life.

A small and very simple word, 'gratitude' can open many doors in your life which you may have felt were closed to you. The possibilities that gratitude can offer you, and the abundance it can bring you is enormously powerful.

We need to open to the possibilities that gratitude can bring us. Gratitude is more than an emotion; it is an important tool for living in a more abundant world. It is a key to having a more joyful existence on this earth. There are wonderful benefits to your emotional, spiritual, and physical life. If you would let gratitude into your life.

If you want to awaken a deeper quality of life, then cultivating an attitude that is positive and seeped in gratitude will do the trick! My experience is the more grateful we are, the happy we become.

There have been many studies in the world to understand the effects of living a grateful live. Some state that you will be more joyful and may find appreciation in all things, big or small. Gratitude can build your self-confidence and when you are more confident, you will also become friendlier.

Others have reported less anxiety and insomnia which helps them have a greater quality of sleep, which is ultimately essential for your health and mental wellbeing.

People have found one of the most vital benefits is that they find they are "awake" or "more present" of their surroundings. Their mindset becomes calmer, and they have trust that all will work out. A positive outlook on life is something we all can use to benefit our daily lives.

Another psychological benefit some have found is that living a life of gratitude helps with their resilience. Without resiliency you may find negative situations beat you down and it takes you forever to come back from them. Challenges are a part of our lives, and we should be able to work through them, not have those challenges crush our self-esteem and sense of worthiness.

The Harvard Medical School published a fabulous article called, 'Giving Thanks Can Make You Happier'.

To quote a short except of the article (which everyone should read!) is the following.

"Gratitude is a thankful appreciation for what an individual receives, whether tangible or intangible. With gratitude, people acknowledge the goodness in their lives. In the process, people usually recognize that the source of that goodness lies at least partially outside themselves. As a result, being grateful also helps people connect to something larger than themselves as individuals – whether to other people, nature, or a higher power."

So then, if you find it hard to have gratitude in your life, this book from the Women Like Me Community members will help. These women have shared their words of gratitude with you so they may help you on your path to feeling more grateful in your life.

Powerful real-life experiences being shared with you, in the hope that you will find more gratitude in your life. I personally am sincerely grateful for each woman who took the time to share words of gratitude with all of us.

The Women Like Me Community – Julie Fairhurst is a Facebook group of like-minded women. Women who want to pay it forward and lift others up and promote healing in the world. Ages ranging from 17 to 83 years of age from all over the world and all walks of life.

I am honored to have the opportunity to get to know them and read their words of gratitude.

If you are interested in our group, you are most welcome and maybe you will participate in one of our community books in the future.

Julie Fairhurst

...

ALEXANDRA KATEHAKIS

"Summoning gratitude is a sure way to get our life back on track.

Opening our eyes to affirm gratitude grows the garden of our inner abundance, just as standing close to a fire eventually warms our heart."

PART 1

SHARING WORDS OF GRATITUDE

1

JENNIFER SPARKS

LEARN TO FLOURISH WHEN YOU ARE NOT IN CONTROL

"Incredible change happens in your life when you decide to take control of what you do have power over instead of craving control over what you don't." — Steve Maraboli

On December 31, 2011, I experienced something I will never be able to blink away. I watched as my twelve-year-old daughter convulsed, turned blue, and stopped breathing on the floor of our living room.

Time stood still. I heard my blood whoosh through my ears. I became a helpless observer. This simply couldn't be happening to us; she was fine only a moment ago.

I remember the exact moment when I realized that I was thinking that my daughter was dead.

I will never forget that choking fear that everything in my life had just changed forever. Nothing mattered at that moment other than her. I begged her to breathe for me. I needed her to breathe. Fear dug in hard and wouldn't let me go.

After several moments of stillness, she took a very slow breath and then another. Her eyes were vacant and staring beyond me. Her arms and hands still twisted beneath her chin, against her chest. It would be hours before she would know who I was.

Little did I know this was the beginning of an unimaginable journey.

While I would lose her to a neurological condition and medication side effects over the next four years, we would also learn and grow together, find happiness in the little things, and learn how to deal with the things we couldn't control.

She was diagnosed with Epilepsy within a few weeks. I was hopeful we could manage this and get on with life. We followed her doctor's orders diligently, and I was meticulous with her medications.

She had more seizures. We increased her medications. We changed her diet. I sought out alternative health practitioners and healers.

Time had a way of slipping by, first in days, then months, and soon years had drifted by without me noticing. We went to the best hospital in the United States, and we were told there was nothing more we could do. This was not what I could accept. Instead, I continued to hope.

Her seizures increased. She couldn't learn. She slept all the time. Depression and anxiety followed.

Her medication side effects were brutal, and I didn't even recognize my daughter anymore. Her beautiful spirit had retreated, held hostage there by the thirty anti-seizure pills she took each day. I knew I couldn't give up on her.

As her primary caregiver, I was sleep-deprived, anxious, terrified, and living in fear of the next seizure. She got worse, and I was drowning because I couldn't control any of it. She required care, supervision, and support that I felt I had no idea how to provide.

One evening, I woke to find her having a Grand Mal seizure in her bed. I sat alone in the dark with her, crying, because I had nothing left to give. I had no way to help her. I had done everything I could, and it still was not enough. I couldn't change things.

I crawled into bed with her so I could watch her breathe. Exhaustion settled over me, but I awoke with a shot of adrenalin when she began to seize violently against me. Again, I begged her to breathe.

I crumbled in the fatigue and the stress and knew that something had to change, or we were going to be totally destroyed by this.

Surrender your desire to control.

At that moment, I knew that I had to surrender my desire to control the uncontrollable. I had tried for four years to manage things beyond my control. The choice got me nowhere and stole my energy faster than I could refuel. I was now absolutely depleted.

I had to come to terms that I couldn't control how long this beautiful child would have on earth. I could not breathe for her. I couldn't watch her every single moment. This was not for me to determine.

This was the hardest thing I have ever had to do, but it made the greatest impact on my well-being, and ultimately hers because I was able to show up differently for her.

In fact, while focusing on my daughter's health, my son was hit by a car while riding his bike. This was a walk-up call to me that trying to control the uncontrollable was nothing but an enormous energy leak.

I couldn't control the seizures, the side effects, or the memory loss. But I could control where I allowed my energy to flow.

Shift your focus.

I decided instead to shift my focus. I could control her schedule. I could make certain she got her medications.

I could get her to the doctor's appointments and scans. I could be supportive and give her my time. I could help her see moments of joy. I could help her with schoolwork. I could be her advocate at school. I could give her more of what she needed between seizures.

As I began to focus my energy on the things I could control, I regained some purpose.

I felt more energized. My hope returned. I was less depleted and more strategic. I began to see new options and opportunities where before my fatigue saw nothing but closed doors. I felt a significant shift. I was spending my limited energy stores in a different way.

Practice gratitude

The other thing I did was I began to practice gratitude.

When you have something so massive pressing down on you, it becomes very hard to not be focused on that. We had been focused on her being sick. We fed the fears. We lived in anticipation of the next catastrophe. We forgot that we still had much to be grateful for.

I began to look for things every day that brought me joy: the sun on my face, a warm cup of creamy coffee, or hearing my kids laughing in the other room. The more I looked for these lovely slivers of joy and hope, the more I saw them.

Soon, I was focused on how blessed I felt and the joy that had always been around me but that I failed to see when I was looking the other way. Even in times of struggle, I continued to look for these simple things, and they were always there for me. I just had to decide to see them.

What this personal struggle ultimately taught me is that letting go of what you cannot control is hard but holding on to these uncontrollable things and trying to manage them is much harder. My energy was best spent on things that could bring me desirable outcomes, not on trying to hold the wind in an open hand.

Our journey has taught me that I am in control of my thoughts, and when I puck my thoughts carefully, I can still flourish in challenging circumstances.

Over four years have passed since this journey began, and I am pleased to say that my daughter has recently enjoyed several years virtually seizure-free.

We have begun to reduce her medications and introduce homeopathic medicine into her daily care. I am hopeful, energized, and optimistic about her future.

There is no doubt in my mind that had I not surrendered and let go of the things I could not control, I would never have had the energy and focus to continue our fight for a seizure-free life.

I know it is hard but letting go of the things you cannot control does not mean you do not care. It means you understand that letting go can lead you to a happier, less stressful life.[1]

---

1. Originally published in Tiny Buddha. Copyright: Jennifer Sparks. Published with permission.

MAYA ANGELOU

"Let gratitude be the pillow upon which you kneel to say your nightly prayer.

And let faith be the bridge you build to overcome evil and welcome good."

2

LINDA FOOTE
YOUR ABCS OF GRATEFULNESS

There is always something you can find to be grateful for. Take a moment and look and see all the gifts the universe gives us. Gives to you! Look in your home or go outside and see what is already at your fingertips. Nature, the birds chirping, flowers in a garden, a beautiful sky. It's all there, and it is FREE for the looking! Take a walk and see what is around you and take it in. Breathe! Be grateful you are alive! Be grateful and appreciate the little things in life.

Being grateful for what you have and what you will receive is so easy if you take a moment to notice.

About four or five years ago, I started a Joy Journal. I would write down what I was grateful for and add quotes that appealed to me. I would often sit with a cup of tea and reread a few of what I have written down; it always makes me feel good. Sometimes it brings back memories.

So, try it, take a moment with a cup of tea, and reread your past writings. I promise it'll promote positivity and a joyful feeling when you do this. It's like creating your own calm.

I start each day with an attitude of gratitude as Jack Canfield would say. Start your day being grateful and live an attitude of gratefulness every day

Here is my 26 days of Gratefulness. I thought it would be fun to pull some of my 'I am Grateful lines' and put them in alphabetical order.

Your ABCs of Gratefulness!

A. I am Grateful for all the Abundance I am receiving in my amazing life. I am living a rich and fulfilled life.

B. I am Grateful for the Beauty that surrounds me from the Universe every day. God is sending Blessings!

C. I am Grateful for the new Confidence, and Courage I see in myself.

D. I am Grateful for living my Dream.

E. I am Grateful for my Essential Oils when I need them.

F. I am Grateful for being Fabulous and Fearless.

G. I am Grateful for my lovely Grandchildren who are so talented and smart.

H. I am Grateful for many things that bring me Happiness and good Health, I am Humble for all I am receiving.

I. I am Grateful for all the Inspiration I see every day.

J. I am Grateful for everything that brings me JOY.

K. I am Grateful for the unconditional Kindness that I've been shown by my friends.

L. I am Grateful to be the Light and Love in someone's life.

M. I am Grateful for my wonderful Marriage.

N. I am Grateful for the Next chapter in my life.

O. I am Grateful for all the Opportunities that come my way.

P. I am Grateful for all the Prosperity and the Positivity that I'm creating in my life.

Q. I am Grateful to live a Quiet and Peaceful life.

R. I am Grateful for living in a Relaxing sunny environment.

S. I am Grateful for the family and friends who Support me.

T. I am Grateful for the Talented and intelligent women in my life the Universe has provided.

U. I am Grateful for living an amazing and Unstoppable creative life.

V. I am Grateful for being able to Visualize my amazing future.

W. I am Grateful for being able to Walk and feel Worthy in my purpose.

X. I am Grateful and XieXie (Thank you in Chinese) to all my lovely friends and family in my wonderful life.

Y. I am Grateful to be able to practice Yoga at my age.

Z. I am Grateful for creating the feeling of Zen where I am manifesting all the wonderful things in my life.

If you haven't started your own Grateful Hour, here are a few tips you might consider trying.

Start a mindful Gratitude practice each morning.

- Set up a happy and comfortable place in your home. A cozy chair or use a yoga mat, whatever makes you feel comfortable.
- Try an essential oil to help create some balance

and create a relaxing mood. Use a diffuser and add a few drops of Doterra Balance Essential Oil. Or you can add a drop of the oil to your pulse points and the bottoms of your feet.

- Grab a cup of tea and your journal.
- Next is music; play some light music, and you could start with this old and lovely song, "Kind and Generous" by Natalie Merchant.
- Follow with 5-minute mindfulness meditation to rejuvenate your spirit.

May this time for yourself bring you a grateful heart full of happiness and joy.

Start a grateful and joyful habit!

...

BRENE BROWN

"What separates privilege from entitlement is gratitude."

3

LORETTA LEBRETON

I've learned that people will forget what you said, people will forget what you did, but people will never forget how you made them feel. —Maya Angelou

I'm very grateful for my five children who have taught me how to be brave and courageous!

I am grateful for my grandchildren who taught me how to be young and carefree and enjoy life through their eyes.

I am very grateful for my dear friend Cindy who has helped me come out of my shell and become something I never thought I could be!

I am grateful that I live in a beautiful country where I am surrounded by mountains, and I get to see the beauty of Mother Earth every everyday! I'm grateful for my freedom that so many have fought for us to have.

I am very grateful for the woman I have become over the last few years.

...

JOHN MILTON

"Gratitude bestows reverence....changing forever how we experience life and the world."

4

LEANNE GIAVEDONI

"When you are grateful, fear disappears, and abundance appears." — Anthony Robbins

When I first started a gratitude practice many years ago, I didn't really know what to put on my list each day.

I started with gratitude for the things I had in my life - my kids, my loving and supportive husband, and my home. Then I started to shift my focus to things I was grateful for about myself.

But something shifted in me and my life when I started to focus on being appreciative for the 'bad and ugly' stuff in my life. This may sound odd, but by finding a gift in the struggle and despair I was released from their grip on me.

So yes, I am grateful that in spite of being molested by my grandfather, and losing my brother to murder, and nearly going bankrupt because of my business failures and dealing with burnout.

I am a strong, loving, forgiving and compassionate woman. I am grateful that I am not defined by the events in my life. I am grateful that I no longer give from an empty cup.

I am grateful that I have opportunities to share that wisdom and courage with others so that they too can manifest a life that they love. I am grateful for the kaleidoscope of experiences in life.

...

ISRAEL AYIVOR

"A sincere attitude of gratitude is a beatitude for secured altitudes. Appreciate what you have been given and you will be promoted higher."

5

PAULINE AWINO ATITWA

"Wherever there is God we are more than winners in our life." — Lilian Mukonyi

Hello to women all over the world!

Life is like an examination day and time at school. Remember that you have to focus forward and never backward in life.

Life is yours; life is you. If you have difficulty in your life, in any situation remember that being grateful will help.

We women are of God, and we are blessed with a spiritual life.

I am grateful for becoming a pastor of a wonderful church in Western Kenya, Kakamega Mumisa. I have a beautiful congregation of women, men, and young and old ones. I am thankful for my life and all that I have.

I am especially grateful for my relationship with God. Be blessed. It is good to have our spiritual life.

...

WILLIAM SHAKESPEARE

"They do not love, that do not show their love."

6

SHERON CHISHOLM

"Rejoice always, pray continually, give thanks in all circumstances, for this is God's will for you in Jesus Christ." — Thessalonians 5:16-18.

I am most grateful for God in my life and for Jesus giving His life for me. There are times I remember during childhood when I felt lost, and Jesus gave me direction in my life.

I am grateful for my mother, for the short time she lived, 58 years. She was an amazing role model. She never complained, even when ill with breast cancer. She stayed strong and relied on God.

I relied on Jesus for answers about many things: what should I do with my life, understanding why I never had the opportunity to be married when I really wanted children, and the direction of my career. I also have gratitude for the times that were not so successful but were blessings I learned from.

One of the things I am most grateful for is my long, full career during which I had many opportunities to succeed in caring for individuals and families; sharing my faith, writing professionally, and speaking nationally and internationally, perseverance to start my own business, and many other things.

The most wonderful, difficult job that I am grateful for is the opportunity to be a mother of three by adoption even though I was never married.

I know I made lots of mistakes, and there were many times I cried out to Jesus for help, but they had a childhood full of opportunities that prepared them for life. They are now grown, married, and making their own way in life.

...

DAN BUETTNER

"Gratitude always comes into play; research shows that people are happier if they are grateful for the positive things in their lives, rather than worrying about what might be missing."

7

JANICE RENSHAW

"When you are grateful, fear disappears, and abundance appears." — Anthony Robins

Years ago, I would spend time being grateful for the material things in my life. I thought this was the most important thing to be grateful for, and today I hear and see so many others doing the same.

In 2010, everything I was grateful for changed and I became even more focused on my physical body and all of its amazing functions that help me to navigate day to day.

I suffered from a detached retina and the possibility of losing my sight in the right eye, was a very scary time. It was this experience that changed how and what I am grateful for from that day forward.

Like many, I took my physical body for granted and it changed that day in February of 2010. I am grateful for my eyes and everything that my body does because without all of these functions, nothing else matters.

Take time everyday to feel your heart beating on its own, your feet and legs that move you forward, your hands that help you to hold your loved ones, your eyes to see, your ears that allow you to hear.

The list goes on and on. Our bodies are an amazing machine that houses our soul.

Look in the mirror and love everything about you and be grateful for it. This can be challenging, but if gratitude doesn't start with you and your amazing gifts the other material things are not important.

I inspire you to hold space and gratitude for the amazing body that keeps you alive to enjoy everyday, and say I LOVE YOU just the way you are.

The rewards are 10-fold, and you will begin to notice that you are inspired to start taking action towards a better, healthier, peaceful you.

...

HANNAH WHITALL SMITH

"The soul that gives thanks can find comfort in everything;
the soul that complains can find comfort in nothing."

8

KIM KORBLE
FAMILY IS WHAT YOU MAKE IT.

I am grateful for many things, but the one thing I can tell you is when the village of people who came in my life to help me with my youngest daughter.

These people who were friends who became family, or the ones who became friends.

For the people who stood by when I thought I had no one.

Without the help of them my life would not be as good.

So, thank you to my village!

...

PRAVIN AGARWAL

"Count your blessings as the more you are grateful for
what you have the more there is to be grateful for."

9

BARBARA KISILOSKI

"Gratitude makes sense of our past, brings peace for today, and creates a vision for tomorrow." — Melody Beattie

I believe being grateful is the experience of counting one's blessings each and every day.

It is a feeling that makes you smile, being mindful and taking the good things out of each day no matter how difficult the day might be.

Open your eyes and mind to the beauty that surrounds you and trust in your path.

I am grateful for the people who are in my life that bring my life joy and for the ability to lead a healthy, active lifestyle.

Never let the things you want make you forget the things you have.

...

LAILAH GIFTY AKITA

"Embrace every new day with gratitude, hope and love."

10

ANNE-MARIE HARRIS

"Gratitude is the sign of noble souls." — Aesop

Gratitude isn't just something to think about, or place to arrive at, it is a lifelong practice.

Gratitude brings you into the present moment, heightening your awareness of self, in a state of mindful observation of the world around you.

I know that I am in control of my thoughts. My mind has the power to heal my heart and spirit. Everyday I respect all that I am capable of by giving thanks to my body for its mobility, to my mind for its strength, to my breath for its life, and to my heart for its light.

Cultivating gratitude has created space for my physical and mental health to improve, my joy and optimism have elevated, and personal connections have become deeper and more meaningful as they continue to expand beyond my imagination. This is what the magnificent art of appreciation can do.

My gratitude practice has assisted my healing journey through pain, trauma and fear. It's rewired my brain to experience my life with a greater sense of purpose, empathy for myself and others, seeing the world through a more compassionate lens. Now when I face challenges, I am able to anchor myself with a tone of deeper grace, ease and understanding.

I'm grateful for the pains, challenges, and struggles; for they continue to make my life full of richness, depth and meaning, reminding me of how truly empowered I am.

This moment. This heartbeat. This breath. This is the gift of the present, and the perfect opportunity to be grateful because it is the first - of the rest and best of your life!

...

STEPHEN RICHARDS

"Gratitude is a form of worship in its own right, as it implies the acceptance of a power greater than yourself."

11

MARISA LAVALLEE

"Be thankful for what you have; you'll end up having more. If you concentrate on what you don't have, you will never, ever have enough." — Oprah Winfrey

Life is a beautiful gift; gratitude is realizing this. There are so many benefits to practicing gratitude daily.

When we are in a place of contentment and are thankful for all that we have and all that we are, everything seems to flow effortlessly for us.

When I was a young girl, I lived in a few places that didn't have running water. To this day I give thanks every time I have a shower.

If we are thankful for the basics like a warm bed to sleep in and food in our bellies, our day will just get better.

Another benefit to being grateful is, that it keeps us in a healthy state of mind. When we are grateful, we are happy and content. Gratitude offsets stress and anxiety and helps us feel safe and secure. Being grateful makes us more balanced, happy, and positive.

If you make practicing gratitude daily, I am certain this will be your most blissful habit.

...

DEBASISH MRIDHA, MD

"If you have peace in your heart, then you will find that the whole world is peaceful."

12

TRISH SCOULAR

"Gratitude turns what we have into enough, and more. It turns denial into acceptance, chaos into order, confusion into clarity… it makes sense of our past, brings peace for today and creates a vision for tomorrow."
— Melody Beattie

I always thought I was a grateful person until my life faced some tough and traumatic times, this was a true test of my character. A demeanour that changed from positive to negative, who felt jealousy, envy and focused on what I felt lacked.

In looking back at my life, I never lacked in anything, I felt loved, provided for, cared about and had jobs that provided an income and enjoyed. Yet in these darkest hours I could not think of one time in my life that was really good.

Instead, I felt, hate, sadness, loss, unloved, poor, and dwelt on, what could possibly be wrong with me to have all this bad luck?

It took years of finally figuring out the problem was not me even though I had lessons to learn, but the people I found myself spending time with who made me feel that I was worthless, never good enough and that I lacked in everything.

Self-love and compassion did not come easy because those beliefs started to stick, becoming construed and confusing. The more I chose to find my way back to those times I felt joy, the more I started to fight those beliefs which made finding gratitude much easier.

...

NATALIE GRACE SMITH

"To better your day, every day - practice gratitude before doing anything else."

13

LINDA S. NELSON

"The single greatest thing you can do to change your life today would be to start being grateful for what you have right now." — OPRAH WINFREY

I honestly owe my present life - a life filled with joy and meaning that I worked hard to create to the simple practice of gratitude. And not just being aware and thankful for what I have - but actually taking intentional, purposeful time each day to be in silence and reflection, taking time to notice and express thanks each day and write it down.

It wasn't always so. I learned through long seasons and tough times that I could find joy in the present - despite my current situation. And I owe it all to the power of gratitude.

One such time was a deep season of depression that lasted years. That's when I started the practice because nothing else seemed to work.

I woke up each day and wrote -- maybe just one thing I was thankful for. I started out with a phrase - a word - a doodle -- anything that could help me find joy in the darkness. Some days I struggled to even find one thing - but gradually - over time with practice and consistency - I began to understand the profound depth of meaning to my life this simple practice brings.

And now - my life has come full circle - and I'm blessed to be able to work with some amazing women to develop this practice in their lives too. And I am blessed beyond anything I could imagine - just because I developed this simple practice.

I hope you're encouraged to start today.

...

LISA J. MORRIS

"Dwelling in the web of regret doesn't change the past.
However, any amount of gratitude can change the present
of how you view the circumstances that you are in."

14

BRENDA COOPER

"Make it a habit to tell people, 'Thank you.' To express your appreciation sincerely and without the expectation of anything in return. Truly appreciate those around you, and you'll soon find many others around you. Truly appreciate life, and you'll find that you have more of it."
— Ralph Marston

GRACEFUL GRATITUDE[1]

A life that is lived on the paths that were chosen
Some were so clear yet some were so frozen
Were the paths that you took made out of fear
Or forged by family and all you held dear

Reflect for a moment about things in your life
Was there internal peace or many a strife
Did you stop and look at the beauty abound
Did you see the wonders that were all around

Gratitude is an immeasurable emotion
It can fill your soul like an elixir or potion
Can you recognize what you are grateful for
Step forward and look and open the door

Thanking yourself is where it begins
Generosity starts from deep within
Appreciate yourself for all of your good
From where you are now and once you stood

Do something kind, show them your grace
Thank someone dear with a joyful embrace
Be grateful for all the small things you give
Be thankful for the life that you can live

Remember those who are less fortunate than you
Remember to do all that you can do
A thankful smile goes a long way
Say thank you to someone every day

Gratitude is nature's special gift
It keeps you grounded so you won't drift
Share it freely and you will see
It will gently enfold you and set you free

1. Copyright Brenda Cooper. Used with permission.

...

VANESSA AUTREY

"Gratitude is a form of surrender. It is a way of saying: I am enough, I have enough, and my life is enough."

15

DONNA FAIRHURST

"Acknowledging the good that you already have in your life is the foundation of all abundance." — Eckhart Tolle

Gratitude: The Principle Giving and Open to Receive Gratitude is energetic tool of choice, designed to be reciprocal in every way.

Choosing a positive appreciative attitude contributes to our greater awareness, balance, and happiness. Many acknowledge the benefits of a daily gratitude process yet struggle to maintain it.

We often choose to see only what is broken, undone, or lacking in our lives. In doing so, we judge ourselves, others, or a situation, thus creating more chaos and incoherence.

It is not a matter of ignoring pain, or injustice in our world. It is rather, the focus we give to it and how we express and deal with it, from a place of calm, coherence, gratitude, and love, thus providing the opportunity to know, grow, flow, and glow, aligned with our highest level of BEING!

It's easy to be grateful for the good things in our lives. When we give ourselves the daily opportunity to acknowledge what is good, stretch our souls to interpret the lessons where we feel there to be lack, we access higher levels of abundance through gratitude, on every level of our being.

Gratitude is a spiritual muscle that grows stronger the more you use it. It will carry you through any trial, or tribulation, if only you use it. It stretches your soul to make more room for abundance, joy, love, purpose, and peace.

Namaste

...

CHARLES F. GLASSMAN

"When you awaken in the morning and go to sleep at night, acknowledge with gratitude the roof over your head and the warm bed upon which you lay."

16

SABRINA LAMBERT

"Any day above ground is a good day. Before you complain about anything, be thankful for your life and the things that are still going well." — Germany Kent

It was Deja Vu. Back in a hospital bed for the second time in my life, I awaited details about my condition.

As the surgeon came to discuss my pending operation, my husband supportively squeezed my hand, yet the furrows in his forehead betrayed his worry. The surgeon looked younger than I expected. So, I secretly hoped that meant he had the most current knowledge about my disease and the skill to best remedy the hot mess inside my abdomen.

Mitigating expectations, the doctor explained, "Until I get a look at what needs to be removed, I won't know if there is enough organ to reattach, and an external appliance could be required."

The thought of a colostomy could not become my focus prior to surgery. Instead, I felt blessed to have access to excellent medical care and my skilled surgeon.

"My preference would be not to need one," I said. "However, I trust you to make the best decision once you see inside. I will be grateful to get well and enjoy my life again, either way."

The doctor nodded and seemed satisfied that I understood the possible outcomes. His smile reassured me that he expected it to go well.

My toughest experience with this surgery was observing the angst and fear my husband suffered on my behalf.

Nine hours later, I awoke in recovery. Although groggy and attached to the many tubes strictly designed to support healing, I knew, gratefully in my core, that all would be well.

KELLI RUSSEL AGODON

"In the beauty of whitecaps, I sometimes see sadness, sometimes how lucky we are to watch the sunrise one more time."

17

DANA K. CARTWRIGHT

"Gratitude is the sweetest thing in a seekers life - in all human life. If there is gratitude in your heart, then there will be tremendous sweetness in your eyes."
— Sri Chinmoy

When I feel gratitude, things change within me and around me.

My heart is lighter, my brain relaxes, a sense of clarity swarms in.

My voice is softer- tone sweeter.

I see differently, I listen more intently, the sounds of nature are heard more clearly.

My muscles relax and every cell in my body is calm.

I love deeper, I laugh louder; pure joy is felt.

It is my most favorite emotional state to reside.

I want to be in it all the time because in gratitude, life becomes simple, easy and oh so sweet! Gratitude nourishes one's mind, body and soul even in its simplest form.

Take time to pause and reflect on your most grateful moments in life and write down the benefits your heart feels.

Soak in the gratitude magic and stay there as long as you can.

...

KRIS FRANKEN

"Your inner voice is subtle, positive, consistent, and peaceful; it springs to life when you pay attention to it, when you show gratitude and trust what's coming through."

18

ERICA DENNIS

"Gratitude turns what we have into enough."
— Melody Beattie

In my mind, Gratitude is gentle. She is soft-spoken, perhaps, with silk-spun hair and velvet lips, two palms made of pillows.

Gratitude is personal, an individual creature that has burrowed in this heart, settling with whispered thanks. And as appreciation comes and goes, I strive to always remember her ardently, to recall the curves of her skin, even when she remains absent in the flesh.

She reminds me to be thankful for my mother, the hands that hindered my fear, that fed me when I wasn't brave enough to eat.

For my father, the arms that held me upright, that became my safe place when I began to weep.

The individuals who anchored me despite my tendency to float.

I feel Gratitude, gentle, and certain, appreciating my forgiving heart, who bears no grudges on my dizzy brain. There are no rules to what one can be grateful for.

Perhaps in your mind, Gratitude is strident. With iron armour, knuckles wrapped to shadow box silhouettes of heed. Gratitude is personal, a creative creature who is unique in each appreciation, thankful with sundry diversity.

You might admire art, find lightness in ink-black coffees, or comfort in purring cats. Appreciation comes and goes, but eventually, Gratitude burrows into your heart, and settles.

...

SHUNYA

"Give and take is the way of the world. But when you give
something with compassion and take something with
gratitude, you are away from the world and
nearer to the supreme power."

19

SHERI GODFREY

"Be thankful for what you have; you'll end up having more. If you concentrate on what you don't have, you will never, ever have enough." — James E. Faust.

When your feet hit the floor in the morning are you alive with excitement or exhausted with overwhelm, stress and anxiety? I can not recall the who or the when but I can recall the what, the words that were bestowed upon me.

Truth be told I don't even recall the situation or what had me in a dark place begrudging the day and the mess I was wading through.

The words of magic bestowed to me are " Someone went to bed last night with plans and expectations for today and sadly, their eyes did not open - they did not get the chance to see a brand-new day - how lucky are we to be here!"

Each day when my feet hit the floor, I try to be mindful, to be grateful, that the Good Lord saw fit to gift me another day on earth.

I have a brand-new opportunity to change my path, shift my mindset and be better then I was yesterday.

Admittedly some days are easier to appreciate then others! If today is one of those tough days, try this: close your eyes softly, breathe in and breathe deep, exhale all of the grey clouds out of your body and breathe in again feeling the warmth of sunshine fill your glorious body.

Take another pause and be grateful that today your eyes opened, your feet hit the floor YOU all of YOU has been gifted a brand-new day.... now go seize it!

...

MATTHEW MCCONAUGHEY

"It's a scientific fact that gratitude reciprocates."

20

THERESA CROWLEY
I AM GRATEFUL FOR EVERYTHING I HAVE

Give thanks for a little and you will gain a lot.

There are a lot of things that are actually out of our control but being grateful is not one of them.

We are totally in charge of our gratitude, large or small. The more that you can praise your life the more we can give praise to others.

I often ask people to listen to music, you not only hear it, but you can feel it. It can take you to another time, and the feelings that surround the music are unique to you.

Oh, how we should recognize and rejoice in our uniqueness.

We acknowledge our feelings, and we are grateful these memories are ours. All it takes is a little unselfish time, a little time to be our true self with love in our heart.

Being grateful is a lot like music, you can hear it and you can feel.... gratitude.

...

STEPHEN D. EDWARDS

"Focusing on what we lack is like seeing garbage all over our blessings."

21

LYNDSEY SCOTT

"Sometimes the smallest step in the right direction ends up being the biggest step of your life." — Naeem Callaway

What does Gratitude mean? Well according to the Oxford Languages grat-i-tude means the quality of being thankful; readiness to show appreciation for and to return kindness.

Gratitude at times can be like a foreign language to me. I have always struggled to truly know and understand the meaning.

Today as I sit here processing the unknown of yet another event to unfold in my journey of this book called LIFE. I realised that Gratitude is very similar to being Thankful.

Now, this is a language I can understand. As every day that passes by no matter how dark my day may be, I will always be thankful for my Children as they are a huge part of the journey I am on.

I am thankful for the experiences I have endured, because without these I would not be who I am today. A woman who loves with all her heart and offers my story to those around me in hopes that it may help even just one person know that they are not alone.

Because even on my hardest days I will always find something in the moment, the day or week that I am Thankful for.

...

MARY DAVIS

"Peace is the answer. Joy is the goal.
Thanks is the prayer. Love is the road."

22

SUSAN DABORN

"The most powerful weapon against your daily battles is finding the courage to be grateful anyway."
UNKNOWN

I am grateful for everyday that I get through, for friends who don't judge me and kind neighbours.

I'm grateful for all the little things in life like the birds or finding a parking spot.

I'm grateful for my dogs and cats who love me unconditionally even when I'm being a jerk.

I'm grateful for the seniors that I care for who keep me humble and grounded.

I'm grateful for the beautiful home I have and the wonderful community I live in, and to be able to share my passion for gardening with others in the community.

There is just so much to be grateful for everyday big or small.

...

CHARMAINE J. FORDE

"True happiness is not money in the bank nor a luxurious home. True happiness is a forgiving heart filled with love and gratitude."

23

MICHELLE VOYAGEUR

"Enjoy the little things, for one day you may look back and realize they were the big things." — Robert Brault

How do I know if I have become a grateful person? This is an easy question for me to answer.

Every morning, the first thing I do is to give thanks for all that I have. It may not be much by some standards, but I have everything I could ever want.

All my daughters live very close to me, which makes visiting easy. I am grateful for my girls, all of whom are extremely close to one other and to me. They have blessed me with three beautiful grandchildren, plus I also have my 'honorary' grandchildren.

What is an honorary grandchild? These are the children of my daughters' friends. Every time I hear, "look, it's Grandma Michelle!" it warms my heart.

Through it all, I must acknowledge my (foster) Mom. Without her, I'm not sure I would've turned out the way I have. She showed me what unconditional love is and how to be nurturing, thoughtful, thankful and especially, grateful.

For these gifts, I cannot thank her enough. It paved the way for how I wanted to build my own family and to fill it with amazing friends.

I have an appreciation for the small things in my life, as they have shown me that deep down, they were big things.

...

MAXIME LAGACE

"As you get wiser, you'll realize how lucky you are for everything that happens for you."

24

COLINDA LAVIOLETTE

"Acknowledging the good that you already have in your life, is the foundation for all abundance." — Eckhart Tolle

I have six sons that I am grateful for. My youngest two sons were born with Down syndrome.

I am grateful for all the blessings, gifts, they have brought with them into this life that have hugely enriched mine and my children's lives.

They have taught us so much about patience, pure unconditional love, full compassion, nonjudgment, understanding, to slow down and fully take in and enjoy life and all it's wonders.

I am grateful for my first four sons, the love, understanding, care, patience, time, that they show and give to their two younger brothers, is always nothing short of amazing.

Without my four older children, their immense love and care for their brothers, their gentleness, the help they provide me from time to time with their little brothers, life would not be as manageable as it is with two little ones who have special needs.

...

TONMOY ACHARJEE

"One of the easiest ways to feel better off is to think what we have and have gratitude for it."

25

KIM MALLORY

"Breathe in gratitude, exhale peace."
Unknown

Gratitude is the key to a joyful life, but it comes at a cost.

It's called adversity which is there to teach us the lessons we need to learn, bring us clarity, and put us on our true path. Without adversity there is no gratitude.

Gratitude isn't about money or status but rather finding the joy in the little things because sometimes the little things are all you've got!

The greatest thing I've ever experienced is what I call "The Gratitude Cry." and let me tell you, it is an amazing feeling!

There is nothing better than being in the moment and realizing just how grateful you are and releasing that beautiful energy with tears of joy.

Be thankful for your past because without it you wouldn't be who you are today.

Be grateful for your mistakes so you can have compassion for others.

Be grateful for your trauma so you can relate to those that need to know they are not alone. Your energy body is calling on you to become your higher self through the essence of gratitude.

To transform your life and the lives of others use the gift of gratitude. Evolve and be the light. Live!

...

LIDIA LONGORIO

"Those who find gratitude in the little things find humility in the big things."

26

IRENE SUTHERLAND

"Your heart is hurting, because I'm reminding
you where it is." (From Spirit)

I'm grateful to have learned to be me.

Who I am makes a difference.

To be a woman who recognized her path. To follow her
path with Joy, even in those times of doubt.

Gratitude is not given; it's learned by mistakes and lessons.
To be grateful, is to have learned to be in the moment of
our life, with open eyes. And for that I am grateful.

Eyes wide open moving forward.

...

DR. IVY NORRIS

"I am grateful for Divine friends, healing energy, interconnectedness, firm hugs, soft kisses, moments of contentment, and growing wisdom."

27

HEATHER SCOTT

"No matter how good or bad you think life is, wakeup each day and be thankful for life because every day you wake up is a good day. Someone else somewhere else is fighting to survive." Unknown

It is really hard for me to even begin to say how blessed and grateful I am, yes, every day I wake up is a good day even when it is not.

My Mother is still with us and lights up my life every time I see her. I have two children, ten grandchildren and a great-granddaughter all of who I am truly in awe of.

I am blessed to work for a great company and staff that go above and beyond. I am grateful for a career that has not only kept a roof over my head but also allowed me to help others when needed.

Every day I am thankful for nights that turn into days, family that turn into friends, friends that turn into family and dreams that turn into reality.

...

RACHEL ROBINS

"Saying thanks to the world, and acknowledging your own
accomplishments, is a great way to feel good
and stay positive."

28

JULIE BREAKS

"At funerals, people say things about a dead person
that they should have told them while they were still
alive." — Wayne Gerard Trotman

For many years of my life, I had a difficult time feeling
gratitude, for almost anything. I suppose that comes with
not feeling worthy of having anything to be grateful for. I
could not receive anything from others. I was embarrassed
if I was given a gift or shown any kindness again, because
I did not feel worthy.

What am I grateful for today? So many things.

I am grateful that I did not give up on myself, although
there were many times, I wanted to do just that.

I am grateful for the person I have become knowing that I
am worthy of everything good life has to offer.

I am grateful for my husband, our children, and our grandchildren.

I am grateful for the amazing women in my life, who love and support me.

I am grateful for my past, my present and my future that is coming.

I am grateful for being here, on this earth, at this time in history, with all of you.

...

TONI SORENSON

"If you woke up this morning, you have reason to be grateful. If you lie your head on a pillow tonight, you have reason to give thanks.

Don't take a single day for granted. They run out."

29

GRATITUDE LESSON
LEANNE GIAVEDONI

Gratitude is the number one way to find happiness! No matter what situation you find yourself in, the feeling of gratitude is the fastest way to pivot and create happiness. If you find yourself feeling stressed or hurt, make a point of looking for something you can feel grateful for. When it seems impossible to find something, then look for a lesson and be thankful for what you can learn.

Make a point to start and end your day with gratitude. Initially, this is best done formally by listing everything in your life you have to be grateful for. It can be done in a journal or through apps available on your phone even.

When you first start this list, you may find yourself thankful about things and other people. Although this is needed and a great start, you also need to create a gratitude list that is about you personally.

Sounds basic but with so many people feeling undeserving and unworthy. It is not easy. Specially to do it in the mirror looking at yourself in the eyes. It can also require you to overcome your feeling boastful to say nice things about yourself.

Don't be surprised that when you start doing this for yourself, others start to compliment you then notice how you respond to those compliments

Can you receive them?

Hopefully, this is not difficult for you, but if it is, just keep at it until you feel comfortable and see your beauty. Start with three things about yourself that you are grateful for. If you need some help, think about the things you love to do, the things that you are naturally good at. A great exercise is to ask people close to you what they love about you.

Now this is actually the easy part of gratitude, but not the most effective!

You see, to truly have a heart graced with gratitude, you need to be able to look at all the suffering and struggle that you have endured and feel peace with it.

Equally you need to be able to see the world through those same eyes.

Forgiveness

Even before gratitude, one must find forgiveness. As long as you are carrying negative feelings you are blocking your heart, and it is only affecting you, not those who hurt you. Sadly, carrying negative feelings is harming you more than it is affecting those who hurt you.

Forgiveness does not mean, "What you did is okay." It merely says, "I am not willing to carry around pain in response to your actions." Finding a lesson learned from these most painful situations is even more necessary and can result in powerful healing. The experience becomes a gift, and it is this that you can be thankful for.

Forgiveness Exercise

Create two columns:

Column One: In one column make a list of any situations or people that have been extraordinarily hurtful or toxic in your life.

Column Two: In the second column, find some lessons you can learn as a result of having experienced this.

Sometimes you may need to allow yourself to feel into the positive lessons, try using the judge and jury exercise to reframe them.

The judge and jury exercise is simply imagining you have a variety of people hearing what you have written. Ask yourself would they all see it from the same perspective-of course they wouldn't.

So, write down some possible perspectives.

A couple can be negative but find a few positive perspectives. Pick one that makes you feel better and able to see the lesson or gift in the experience. Now you have something to be grateful for.

In addition, to forgiving others, you need to ultimately forgive yourself.

In some cases, this may be the hardest part! And the reason so many people have such strong feelings of unworthiness or undeserving. Even when you are the victim of the hurt and hardship, somehow the brain can turn that into shame.

Shame being the heaviest form of fear and lowest vibration emotion at the root of so much pain and suffering.

Now, repeat this process, but this time list anything you have done that needs forgiveness.

For each item in column one, say the following:

"I am sorry, I forgive you, I thank you, and I love you."

This comes from a Hawaiian prayer called Ho'oponopono and can be repeated often to help move into a space of forgiveness.

Here is an example:

Situation or Person Who Hurt Me: Being bullied

Positive lesson(s) It Taught Me: To get over what others think of me, to be kind

Something I Need to be Forgiven For: Business failure

Positive lesson(s) It Taught Me: New ways to measure success

Writing all of this out on paper, saying the Ho'oponopono Prayer and then burning the piece of paper is a very powerful releasing experience.

Now, go back to your daily gratitude list and notice that you can expand the things that you feel appreciation for.[1]

----

1. Adapted from Chapter 8 of Fear Unravelled by Leanne Giavedoni with permission.

...

ANNE FRANK

"I lie in bed at night, after ending my prayers with the
words
'Ich danke dir für all das Gute und Liebe und Schöne'
(Thank you, God, for all that is good and dear and
beautiful)"

30

YOUR MINDSET MATTERS
JULIE FAIRHURST

Do you find it difficult to remain in a positive mindset? Sometimes, it doesn't matter how hard you try, your negative thoughts can take over and control what you're thinking about. This happens to all of us, throughout our lives. To change our mindsets, we need to get to work changing our thoughts.

Your thoughts are just a habit you can change.

There are several studies quoted over that state you think an average of 60,000 thoughts per day. Some of those thoughts will pass quickly though your mind and others may linger.

What I find disturbing in these studies is that 70% of the thoughts we are thinking today, are the same thoughts from yesterday and the same thoughts from the day before.

When we are in this negative thought pattern, it is a habit that must be broken to ensure you can live your best life!

You can start to change your thoughts by reciting daily mantras. When a negative repeating thought pops into your mind, find a mantra that you can use to shut it down. The more often you can shut it down, the less you will have it coming back into your thoughts.

A mantra that I use daily, several times a day is…

'I see you, and I release you.'

When I say this out loud to myself, the negative thought floats away. If I'm in an area where I can't speak out loud, then I say it myself in my mind. It's amazing the power this one statement has.

I use it when the old guilt and shame comes up about something that I can't do anything about. I need to forgive by acknowledging it's there and releasing it to the universe. I urge you to try it over a few days and see how much better you will begin to feel.

What you focus on is what you will attract into your life

This makes sense, right?

As you focus your attention on something, good or bad, you are putting your energy into what you are focusing on. And, if this is true, which I 100% believe it is, then why not work on focusing on what you want in life rather than what you don't want.

You're going to focus, you decided where that focus will go.

Worry will just bring you more to worry about and we have enough to worry about in this fast-paced world. Consider what you worry about and decide for yourself if it is worth your time?

I suspect 90% of what keeps you up at night is out of your control. And, if it's out of your control, then it's time to release the worry and open to more positive thoughts. Don't you think?

And now let's focus on gratitude.

Truly one of the most powerful ways to change your negative mindset to a positive one and thus, change your life is the use of gratitude.

Gratitude, being thankful, appreciation, gratefulness, and thankfulness, these are all forms of each other. It doesn't matter what word you resonate with, when used they will help you change your life for the better.

I use the word appreciate when I want to acknowledge others. My husband for example. I tell him how much I appreciate that he cooks dinner or supports me. I tell my friends I appreciate them being there for me. I tell the ladies in my Women Like Me Community how much they are appreciated for all they do.

I like to let the service workers who serve me my food in restaurants how much I appreciate their service. Anyone that helps me during my travels throughout my day, I want them to know that I appreciate what they did for me.

It took a while to work up to telling a stranger how much I appreciated what they did, but, oh the smile on their face warms my heart. We are sometimes so quick to judge others and not so quick to point out a kindness.

Try making lists.

This is something that will really help you open your gratitude mind if you feel stuck.

Let's say you have a co-worker who is getting on your nerves, and you are not getting along. But you must work together everyday. Spend a few minutes and jot down on paper, what you appreciate about this person. For sure there will be something. And then, start to tell that person what you appreciate about them. It doesn't have to be massive; it can be little things. And watch your relationship start to flourish.

The same can be done for your loved ones. If you have difficulties with anyone, focus on what you appreciate, and things should smooth out. And if it doesn't, at least you know you tried all you could and you will feel better about you and the situation.

Your mind is a sponge.

Lastly, I'd like to have you take notice of how your mindset became negative. Where did those negative recurring thoughts come from? We are born perfect little humans, the environment we grow up or live in can certainly affect our mindsets. Negative messages, that we hear about ourselves will become ingrained deep in our souls and can control our behaviour and our life if we don't do something to help ourselves.

What do you watch on TV or what do you listen to? Fill your mind with positives. Don't watch so much news. Listen to positive motivation talks on podcasts or YouTube. Most of it is free so there is no excuse that you can't find something uplifting to listing to.

Find books that inspire and lift you up. Read a little each day to keep you motivated.

What about your friends? How are they effecting your mindset? It's important to protect our mindset from others who are not lifting us up in our life. Limit your time with those and spend more time with those who only want the best for you.

Your family members can be a bit harder if they are in a negative state. But you can do many things to become inspired and motivate yourself.

Choose conversations that are positive and don't let yourself get dragging into the negative. Realize you can not change anyone, only yourself. And that you are responsible for you, your actions, your thoughts, your future, and your life. And others are responsible for themselves.

Changing your mindset is a journey. If you stay on the path, it will work for you. I know it will, it did for me and many others that I know.

Here are some affirmations that you may want to use during your day to fill yourself up with good thoughts and love in your heart. You can write them on sticky notes, place them where you'll see them daily. Make your habit a positive. You can do it; I know you can!

1. I am grateful for my life as it is today.
2. I know I am getting better and better each day.
3. I am appreciative of all the blessings in my life.
4. I am grateful for my family.
5. I am thankful for the lessons of my life.
6. I can do it.
7. I am thankful for this new day.
8. I am grateful to be alive.
9. I appreciate each and every part of me.
10. Today I will have an attitude of gratitude.
11. I am thankful for the growth in my life.
12. I find the good in everyone I meet.
13. I am open to receiving all good things.
14. I attract positive loving people into my life.
15. I am the creator of my life.
16. I always have everything I need.
17. I appreciate I job
18. I accept love and appreciation into my life.
19. I am loved and respected.
20. My world is peaceful and loving.

...

SUSAN BARBARA APOLLON

"Begin your day with gratitude and end your day with gratitude. A heart filled with loving expressions of thanks is a beautiful offering to the universe."

31

CONFIDENCE JOURNAL
FREE GIFT

If you would like to start journal, please accept this gift from me to you. This is my free Confidence Journal. Here you will find links to some of my favourite motivational videos and other valuable tools to help you in your journey of discovery.

Link to the Free Confidence Journal
https://womenlikemestories.com/confidence-journal-free/

32

THANK YOU TO THE WLM COMMUNTIY

My gratitude and appreciation to all the members of the Women Like Me Community Group!

Once again, you ladies have stepped up and shared with the world from deep inside your souls. You have shared your words of gratitude with others.

I know for some of you, it was hard to find gratitude, but you did it and I am proud of each and everyone of you.

Ladies, without you, this book could not have been published. Others need to hear your wisdom. I thank you for this and I know they will as well.

At times we find it difficult due to lives circumstances to find anything to be grateful for. I know this to be true because I was once there, and I know many of you were also there at one time in your life. However, when we let gratitude flow through us, our lives can and do change, for the better.

Writing your words of gratitude in this book is a labour of love. It's women supporting women. I appreciate you all very much.

Not only will your wisdom be shared with those who need to hear it, you are also helping to raise money for breast cancer research with the sales proceeds from this book. This community group of women are truly givers in the world, and it shows here with volume two of our community books.

So, I thank you, I thank all of you for what you've done here and for what you do for our world. It really doesn't have to take a massive amount of effort to make a difference in the lives of others. It is the little things we do daily that makes a difference.

If we do a little something everyday, we can change our world. A little bit at a time.

Let's continue the good work ladies, let's change the world together.

With much appreciation,

Julie

PART 2

LEARN MORE ABOUT WOMEN LIKE ME

33

JOIN THE WOMEN LIKE ME COMMUNITY

If you do not belong to **Women Like Me Community – Julie Fairhurst** I would be pleased if you decided to join us.

The Women Like Me Community – Julie Fairhurst is a Facebook group of like-minded women. Women who want to pay it forward and lift others up and promote healing in the world. Ages ranging from 17 to 83 years of age from all over the world and all walks of life.

As a community we write community books, with the proceeds going to charity. Maybe you will join in on the next book?

Together, as a group, we can help promote healing in our world.

...

SAMA AKBAR

"Love and forgive the person you used to be.
Love and nurture the person you are.
Love and celebrate the person you know you will be."

34

KIND WORDS FROM WLM AUTHORS

Working with Julie on Women Like Me was a truly wonderful experience. She helped me along when I was stuck, she was a cheerleader for me through it all, and was always readily available for any of my concerns or problems. I remember the day the book came out, I was exhilarated, I was published! Anyone that has the chance to go through this process with Julie will come out on the other side a better person and also will be helping many other women who have gone through the same or similar circumstances.

Christine Luciani – Women Like Me Author

I truly appreciate Julie for her patience, encouragement, support and leadership as I wrote the story, tips and suggestions when I kept sending back my editing to her, for her encouragement for me to write my story. I was very impressed how organized Julie is in getting everyone motivated to write, encouragement and patience as we submitted our stories and bios, and how she is looking out for those who are apart of this process that everyone is feeling included and important. *Karla Weiss – Women Like Me Author*

The opportunity to share my story has been a priceless gift. With Julie's support and simple process, I have been able to reach out to so may other women who may otherwise think they face their struggles alone. I have wanted to write professionally for years and Julie has made it possible. The passion she shares is helping women from all over the world and THAT is amazing! *Brenda-Lee Hunter – Women Like Me Author*

I am so grateful for this opportunity to bring my personal story out from the darkness within and shine some light on it. Julie was instrumental in helping me to figure out what it is that I wanted to say by sharing my story. I've always had the hopes of helping others, and she provided a way to do so. Thank you, Julie, for bringing this together for us all.

Jennifer Robertson – Women Like Me Author

Julie was an amazing guide and mentor into the world of authors and their stories. She keeps you focused. She gently pushes you and brings out the best author in you and encourages you throughout the whole process. And although this was all new to me ~ I never felt alone doing it, Julie made sure I knew she would be there anytime I needed her and feeling that safety of knowing her door is always open allowed me the freedom of taking the dive into becoming an author! A best-selling author, no less! *Rhonda Devlin-Gilbert – Women Like Me Author*

Having Julie as a mentor, cheerleader and now, a friend, I would like to know that more women would be willing to take this chance, to not be afraid and to know that anything is possible. Julie knew I could write and with her encouragement, I wrote about my life and felt stronger as I went along. Now I am seeking out other brave women to find Julie and write their stories. How lucky am I? *Michelle Voyageur - Women Like Me Author*

Julie is wholeheartedly connected to her writers and this project. She gave me trust and time when I needed it and supported and celebrated me along the way. She helped me get it out there!!! *Leontine Boxem – Women Like Me Author*

...

ITAYI GARANDE

"Gratitude is what turns what may seem as an intensely painful life into an intensely thrilling adventure."

35

MEET JULIE FAIRHURST

I'm Julie Fairhurst the founder of Women Like Me.

I want to share with you, how Women Like Me came into existences.

When I was 10 years old, my mom killed her best friend in a car accident while driving drunk. Three little girls lost their mom that night. And so, did I. My mom didn't physically die, she died inside and was never the same again.

Her life spiraled down due to shame and unbelievable guilt, and she took her children with her.

Drug addiction and alcoholism became rapid in my family. My siblings and myself were thrown into a life of chaos, it was completely out of control.

For me, I became pregnant at 14 years of age, married at 17 and divorced at 29, a single mother with three young children, and a grade eight education, I thought my life was set for failure, following down my parents' path. I was headed in the wrong direction.

But, somewhere deep inside, that young girl inside showed up and reminded me that I wanted better for my life and the life of my children. I had no support from anyone, not a soul. I had to do it all on my own.

Was it an easy road? No, it was far from easy. I was a single mom for 24 years. We lived off government handouts. I stood in line at food banks to feed my kids. At Christmas, we received Christmas hampers, and I would go to the toy bank to get presents for the kids. The path we were on was not easy to change, especially when it is all that you knew.

But I did it. I went back to school and finished my education. I built an outstanding career, in sales, marketing and promotion. I won the company's top awards and was the first woman to achieve top salesperson year after year, in a male dominated industry. I was able to buy a home on my own and provide a stable environment to raise my children.

Some people would say to never look back, but I do every day. Why? Because I never want to forget the journey that led me to where I am today. And today, my life is entirely different. I didn't just fall into this life. I worked at it, every day, all the time.

Then, in 2019, my beautiful 24-year-old niece died on the streets of Vancouver, Canada from a drug overdose. And that was the day, I said enough! My niece's death was an indirect result of my mothers' actions or non-actions and of my siblings continuing with their destructive lifestyles.

When we don't deal with our traumas, we pass the dysfunction along to the next generation and the next. This is where my passion comes from, the reason I started Women Like Me. But I am only one person.

Now I am reaching out to you, you who would be in service of others, healers, coaches and really anyone who deals with the public in a personal capacity. If you work with the public, you may not think you can help them change their lives, but you can.

I have started a movement, but I can't do it alone. It's time to share your stories with others to inspire change in their lives and to help us all along our way.

...

GZA

"Live a life full of humility, gratitude,
intellectual curiosity, and never stop learning."

36

IS IT TIME FOR YOU TO BECOME A PUBLISHED AUTHOR

The ***Women Like Me Academy*** has been formed to help you get your story out of your heart and head and into a book. Writing a full book is a taunting task and well, it can be so overwhelming that many of us will put writing on the back burner. And most times, it never gets written.

Writing a chapter of your story is a fantastic way to get your story out into the public, where it can be read and inspire others to make changes in their lives. Your chapter story can benefit you in many powerful ways. Let's talk about your story!

Is it time for you to becoming a published author?

Deciding which story of your life to write can be a confusing and daunting task. This alone has stopped many a writer. Not to worry! I excel at helping you draw your story out of your head and heart and getting it onto paper.

Together we can choose which of your life stories is the perfect one to use for the academy. We will have a private conversation to flush out your story, so you feel comfortable opening up about what you feel is the story you want to tell. The story, which will benefit you in your life and help others.

Whether you are or are not a professional writer has nothing to do with you writing your story!

I will be guiding you every step of the way and if you are stuck, we will get you unstuck. Don't worry, I will keep you flowing. There will be editing of your chapter to ensure spelling, punctuation, grammar and that all is correct. You can do this; I know you can!

Becoming a published author gives you an amazing number of tools to use to promote yourself and your story!

By the time we are finished our time together, you will be ready to share your story with the world. And, most importantly, you will gain the distinction of being called a Published Author.

If you would like to learn more about the Academy, you can go here…

https://womenlikemestories.com/women-like-me-academy

...

JODI AMAN

"Give forgiveness, give gifts, give gratitude, give love, give time, give joy, give tears, give hugs, give an ear, give a speech…. Simply give."

37

CONNECT WITH ME

Would you like to connect with me?

If you would like to reach out to me for any reason, I would love to connect with you. Here's how you can find me.

julie@changeyourpath.ca

www.womenlikemestories.com

Follow me on social media:

Facebook:

- Rock Star Strategies:
- www.facebook.com/juliefairhurstcoaching
- Instagram:
- Inspire by Julie:

- https://www.instagram.com/womenlikemestories/
- LinkedIn:
- https://www.linkedin.com.in/womenlikemestories

...

TONY ROBBINS

"If we can realize that life is always happening for us, not to us … game over, all the pain and suffering disappears."

ALSO BY JULIE FAIRHURST

Other Books by Julie Fairhurst can be found on Amazon or on the womenlikemestories.com website:

- Women Like Me Community Messages To My Younger Self (volume one)
- Self Esteem Confidence Journal Build Your Self Esteem - 100 Tips designed to boost your confidence
- Women Like Me - A Celebration of Courage and Triumphs (volume one)
- Women Like Me - Stories of Resilience and Courage (volume two)
- Women Like Me – A Tribute to the Brave and Wise (volume three)
- Women Like Me – Breaking Through The Silence (volume four)
- Positivity Makes All The Difference Your Mindset Matters
- Agent Etiquette - 14 Things You Didn't Learn in Real Estate School
- 7 Keys to Success - How to Become a Real Estate Sales Badass
- 30 Days To Real Estate Action
- Net Marketing
- 100 Reasons Agents Quit

Manufactured by Amazon.ca
Bolton, ON

26014821R00102